D0462082

Lessons from the Monastery That Touch Your Life

M. Basil Pennington, O.C.S.O.

Paulist Press
New York/Mahwah, New Jersey

Cover/book design and interior illustrations by Nicholas T. Markell.

Library of Congress Cataloging-in-Publication Data

Pennington, M. Basil.
    Lessons from the monastery that touch your life / by M. Basil Pennington.
        p.   cm. — (Illuminations series)
    Includes bibliographical references.
    ISBN 0-8091-3515-9 (pbk.)
    1. Spiritual life—Catholic Church.   2. Catholic Church—Customs and practices.   3. Monastic and spiritual life.   I. Title.
    II. Series: IlluminationBooks.
BX2350.2.P432   1994
255—dc20   94-31704
                                                                    CIP

Published by Paulist Press
997 Macarthur Boulevard
Mahwah, New Jersey 07430

Printed and bound in the
United States of America

Contents

IlluminationBooks: A Foreword   v

Welcome   1

Chapter One   6
   "Seven Times in the Day..."
Chapter Two   14
   In the Middle of the Night
Chapter Three   22
   By the Labor of Their Hands
Chapter Four   27
   Let Them Devote Themselves
   to Their Reading
Chapter Five   36
   I Will Refresh You
Chapter Six   43
   The Tranquility of Order
Chapter Seven   49
   Welcome Again

Goodbye for Now   53

IlluminationBooks
A Foreword

*I*lluminationBooks *bring to light wonderful ideas, helpful information, and sound spirituality in concise, illustrative, readable, and eminently practical works on topics of current concern. Learning from stress; interior peace; personal prayer; biblical awareness; walking with others in darkness; appreciating the love already in our lives; spiritual discernment; uncovering helpful psychological antidotes for our tendency to worry too much at times; and important guides to improving interpersonal relations are only several of the areas which will be covered in this series.*

The goal of each IlluminationBook, then, is to provide great ideas, helpful steps, and needed inspiration in small volumes. Each book offers a new beginning for the reader to explore possibilities and embrace practicalities which can be employed in everyday life.

In today's busy and anxious world, Illumination-Books are meant to provide a source of support—without requiring an inordinate amount of time or prior preparation. Each small work stands on its own. Hopefully, the information provided not only will be nourishing in itself but also will encourage further exploration in the area.

One is obviously never done learning. With every morsel of wisdom each of these books provides, the goal is to keep the process of seeking knowledge ongoing even during busy times when sitting down with a larger work is impossible or undesirable.

However, more than information (as valuable as it is), at the base of each work in the series is a deep sense of *hope* that is based on a belief in the beautiful statement made by Jesus to his disciples and in turn to us: "You are my friends." (Jn 15:15)

As "friends of God" we must seek the presence of the Lord in ourselves, in others, in silence and solitude, in nature, and in daily situations. IlluminationBooks are designed to provide implicit and explicit opportunities to appreciate this reality in new ways. So, it is in this Spirit that this book and the other ones in the series are offered to you.

—*Robert J. Wicks*
General Editor, IlluminationBooks

Welcome

A few years ago I was invited to address a meeting of the Center for the Study of Democratic Institutions at the University of California, Santa Barbara. In introducing me the Director said he found it comforting that there were still monks and nuns around. It was like those old tomes on the shelves in the library. Unused though they be, it was good to know they are there.

I must confess, I don't really feel like an old unused tome on the shelf. Nor do I think many, if any, monks or nuns think the purpose for their being around is to be a comfort to the nostalgic. Our reason for being is something much more vital than that and much more intimately united with our fellow humans. Indeed, we are one with all in the creative love of our heavenly Father. And even more deeply one as women and men baptized into Christ, giving expression to his redeeming and much-loved prayer.

If you ask any monk or nun why he or she dwells in the cloister, the first answer will always be: because God wants it. Nothing can be more right and in less need of justification than the fulfillment of the will of God. But we have responded to God's invitation to dwell within, with hearts filled with peace and joy, because such a life has so much meaning to it. We know the privilege of a freedom that allows us to gather in choir, once in the night and seven times in the day, to glorify, praise and thank our all-good God, not only in our own name but in the name of all creation, of the whole human family. We are humbled by the solemn duty to make intercession with Christ for all the needs of the earth, for a humanity which has so many and such pressing needs. We are grateful for the hours of leisure that allow us to listen deeply to the Word of God as it speaks so personally to us in the inspired Scriptures and to rest deeply in the divine, all-embracing Love that dwells in the center of our being.

Prayer is without a doubt what primarily gives meaning to our lives as monks and nuns. In this we are here for God—and for others. But we also have a witness to give. And if it is understood it might give a good bit more consolation to our fellows than those old unused tomes on the library shelf. And it is precisely that which we want to share a bit in this little volume.

What does it say to thoughtful men or women as they perhaps drive along and spy a monastery set on a distant hill or down a verdant valley? And perhaps drive up that hill or into the valley for a bit of a visit? These monks or nuns certainly are apart. They have stepped back from the busyness of the world. There is a quietness, a peace atop this hill, in this valley. It is something more than a country quietness. There is a depth to the peace. It is the climate of monastic prayer.

The posted schedule will quickly tell the visitors that we monastics spend a lot of time in prayer. And that day of prayer begins early, indeed! Maybe as early as 2:15. Or at the midnight hour. The surroundings: from the beautiful landscaping to out across the carefully-tended fields, all bespeak a life that knows its daily labor, a labor loving and attentive.

The guest area: chapel, parlor, garden, retreat house, all beckon the visitor: welcome. You are at home here. You belong to our family. Joyful faces, warm hands say it. There is care for body as well as soul. A wise, compassionate ear, with a wisdom that does not come from this world, is always ready, more to listen than to speak. But there are words, for truly human silence always has its humanity.

It doesn't take the friendly visitor long to discover these things. But let us reflect on them a bit. Let us reflect together. What are the lessons you might draw from a monastery?

* * *

But before we begin our reflections together, let us pause for a moment. Our Teacher said: Wherever two or three are gathered in my name, there I am in the midst (Mt 18:28). As we come together for this reflection, he is with us. Let us turn to him. On the night before he died for us he said: The Spirit, the Paraclete will teach you all things (Jn 14:26). Let us now ask him to breathe forth his Spirit upon us that we might truly profit by these "lessons" and come to enjoy a fuller, deeper, more peaceful life in love.

* * *

Lord Jesus, Son of God, Wisdom of God, be with us now. Breathe forth your Spirit, the Spirit of Love, upon us. May your Spirit help us to truly understand and come to joyfully know something of the peace and the joy and the love that the monks and nuns find in their prayer, in their labor, in their hospitality, in their way of wisdom and serenity. That our lives might be more and more one with yours to the glory of your Father and for the uplifting of the entire human family. Amen.

Father M. Basil, O.C.S.O.

Our Lady of Joy Monastery
Lantau Island, Hong Kong
Birthday of Our Lady, September 8, 1993

Chapter One

"Seven Times in the Day..."

M ost monks and nuns in the English-speaking world live according to the Rule written by a wise old man by the name of Benedict. This saint lived and wrote his Rule in the sixth century–a little while ago! Among his many maxims, Benedict told his disciples that nothing was to be preferred to the Work of God. For the saint, the Work of God par excellence was the chanting of God's praises and making intercession. He takes up the words of the psalms which are so constantly chanted by the monks and nuns: "Seven times in the day I have praised you" (Ps 118 [119]:164).

As the rising sun begins to fill the sky with its promise, the monks gather to praise and thank the Lord for the gift of another day. It is especially a moment for praise, for the rising sun reminds us of the Son who came from on high to enlighten us with the true and eternal light and to guide us in the way of peace. This first of the seven "hours" (though they are more truly just so many minutes—maybe this first hour and the evening hour, the two principal hours, more approach the reality of being an hour of praise) is more than any of the others an hour of praise. The psalms of praise are chosen and run to a climax in the final psalm of the Psalter:

> Praise God in his temple!
>> Praise his strength in heaven!
> Praise him for the mighty things he has done!
>> Praise his supreme greatness!
> Praise him with trumpets!
>> Praise him with harps and lyres!
> Praise him with drums and dancing!
>> Praise him with harps and flutes!
> Praise him with cymbals!
>> Praise him with loud cymbals!
> Praise the Lord, all living creatures! (Ps 150).

And Zachary's joyful canticle is chanted: Blessed be the Lord God of Israel (Lk 1:68-79).

It is only with Prime, the prayer of the first hour, that we turn to petition and call upon the Lord to bless the

day and bless the work of our hands. Today, often enough, monastics combine these two hours, Lauds and Prime, and celebrate them as one morning office.

Terce, Sext and None, the prayers of the third, sixth and ninth hour of the day (9 AM, Noon, and 3PM), are but brief moments of praise and prayer. They give expression to our mindfulness (and renew that mindfulness, if it has slackened) that all that we are receiving as we go through the day is God's most gracious gift: our ability to breathe, to think, to do, to love.

As evening comes, and labors end, we settle into a longer period of thanksgiving. This day has been the Lord's gift, with all its fruitfulness. Before we finish, we take up Mary's exalting and humbly grateful words:

> My soul magnifies the Lord
>   and my spirit rejoices in God my Savior,
>   because he has regarded his servant.
> Behold, from henceforth all will call me blest,
>   because he that is mighty has done great things
>   for me.
> And holy is his name (Lk 1:46-49).

After the joys of a quiet, familial evening, we finally complete our day with the service that is aptly called Compline. There is time to reflect on the day. We, poor sinners that we are, have to express some word of repentance and receive a word of forgiveness that will allow us to sleep with a more peaceful spirit. We pray that while we take our rest, a watchful Love will watch over us and our world. We go to rest in the hope of an even more blest tomorrow. This hour ends with a poignantly beautiful chant, usually sung by candlelight, a good-night hymn to our heavenly mother:

> Hail, holy Queen, Mother of Mercy,
> our life, our sweetness, and our hope....

What a tremendous difference it can make when life is so laced with prayer, above all prayer of praise and thanksgiving. A grateful spirit is a joyful spirit. An ever-present knowledge that a beneficent God is with us through the day takes much of the fear and burden from our hearts. "Cast your care upon the Lord," says Saint Peter, "for he has care of you" (1 Pet 5:7). As he has promised, our God does answer prayer. His answer might not always be understood by us, his children. What child fully understands why a loving parent sometimes seems to turn a deaf ear or say a forceful "no." But it is the same responding love. Loving parents do not let their dear little one play with the carving knife, no matter how much he or she may ask.

In the midst of a care-laden life with all the responsibilities of home and work and community, what can a married person or a single do to celebrate these hours of prayer. To lace their day with the joy and consolation of prayer and praise?

If we set our minds to it, if it is a value we want to incorporate into our lives, it is not that difficult. Remember, God is in eternity, we are the ones in time. Intensity is what matters, not duration. We can develop rhythms or habits that will support us.

As the alarm goes off, even before we stir out from under our covers, we can begin our Lauds: Thank you, Lord, for another day of life. I offer this whole day to you and commit it to your loving care. The "morning offering" might become a habitual part of our rising:

> O Jesus, through the immaculate heart of Mary, I offer you all my prayers, works, joys and suffering of this day, for all the intentions of your sacred heart, in union with the holy sacrifice of the Mass throughout the world, in reparation for my sins and for the intentions of ...

As we go about our exercise, our washing, our dressing, we can continue our prayer and praise. We might put some hymns we like on the cassette or CD player to help set the mood and support our prayer. There are readily available recordings of monks and nuns singing their Lauds. My aunt and uncle pray a psalm together when they get to the breakfast table. A little creativity on our part will find the way that best works for us.

As we head off to work, a prayer of Prime might call down God's blessing on what lies ahead: Bless the work of our hands, O Lord, bless the work of our hands.

Through the day we can have little prayer-breaks. Maybe each time the chime sounds on our watch, we can send a prayer heavenward. Or each time we pass through a certain door or do some repeated task or take a cup of coffee. It is a matter of choosing the time, the helpful association, that will bring us back into consciousness that all that we are and are doing is gift and is gifted with continual watchful care on the part of a God who loves us so.

When we come home in the evening, we know the fatigues of the day. We might sit in a comforting bath or stand under a shower or just sit in a corner to catch our breath. It is a moment when we can offer our Vespers/prayer: Thanks, Lord, for all this day. You have gifted me with life and so much more. Thanks for all you have done this day for all my loved ones, all my co-workers, all my world.

And finally, as we snuggle under our covers, and perhaps settle into the intimate embrace of a loved one, we can take thought of a loving God who holds us in his embrace and gives us all the love that does surround us.

Of course, at any of these times, we can take more than the quickly passing moment and enjoy a fuller time with the Lord. We can have our Bible at hand and open to a psalm. We can invite the Lord to say a word to us through his inspired word.

All this is a beginning of walking more with the Lord as friend: I no longer call you servants, but friends.... I have chosen you. Soon enough we will talk more spontaneously with him about all that is transpiring as we walk along together. No more loneliness for us: Though I walk through the valley of death, you are with me. To be near God is my happiness.

And, yes. With God we will come to love this world of his—and ours—more, and our prayer will be more embracing. We will know that there is something we can do about all the overwhelming needs: we can pray.

Seven times in the day.... Not seven times, but seventy times seven (Mt 18:22).

Chapter Two
In the Middle of the Night

*A*ppealing again to Psalm 118 [119], *this time verse 62: "At midnight I arose to give you praise," Saint Benedict tells his monks and nuns that "we should praise our Creator for his just judgments at these times: Lauds, Prime, Terce, Sext, None, Vespers and Compline; and let us arise at night to give him praise."*

In reflective moments we monks and nuns are not unaware that the "vibes" of our prayer flow out from the monastery into the immediate environs and on, encircling the whole globe in a current of peace and caring love, uniting with the prayer of all and lifting up each one. But in the midst of the prayerful chant we are more conscious of the ascent to God, or rather of God himself and of all that ascends with our prayer. When questioned as to what we are about, we do not usually first think or speak of the empowering and uplifting, though they certainly are important. We know well that when the consciousness of one person is raised, the whole of humanity is raised, when the quality of life of one improves, all improve. Or, to put it in another, more biblical way, the increased health and vitality of any one cell vitalizes the whole Body of Christ.

But we monks think more readily of Jesus and see our rising in the night for prayer as an imitation of our Master. At the significant moments of his life Jesus entered into a watch of prayer. As he inaugurated his healing ministry at Capernaum,

> In the morning, long before dawn, he got up and left the house, and went off to a lonely place and prayed there (Mk 1:35).

When it came time to choose his apostles,

> He went out into the hills to pray; and he spent the whole night in prayer to God (Lk 6:12).

We pray in the night in imitation of our Lord and Master but also because this expresses the very essence of our life. If we listen to what is deepest in us we find a deep longing for God; a mind that seeks all Truth, a desire to know that will be satisfied only when it finds the ultimate Answer that ties everything together. And more important, more urgent, and in the end more profoundly at the center of our being, there is a heart that longs for a limitless love, a heart that seeks that Love who is God himself—the only Love big enough to fill all our void. Indeed, if we listen attentively we hear this seeking deep in every human voice, see it in every human eye; we perceive it in all the restless striving of our sisters and brothers. And in the rest of creation—the whole of creation is in travail, groaning, seeking its fulfillment in the fullness of the redemption that is to come to it.

One of the awesome models for monks and nuns is the great Arsenius. We are told that as the sun set he raised his arms in prayer and did not lower them until the rising sun cast its shadow on the ground before him; then he prostrated before the Risen Son. Not many can approximate this holy monk's steadfastness. Saint Benedict legislated for a weaker lot. He rouses his monks from bed at the seventh hour of the night—around two or three AM—after they are rested. And what do we do at that hour of the night and in the subsequent hours? We watch and wait for the dawn. It is a time of seeking, of longing, of wanting.

Something deep within twists and stretches, taut with longing and expectation. Our watching is the bride's eager straining to catch a glimpse through the lattice of faith or the bridal party's excited listening for the footfall at the door. But there are those dull nights, when a damp chill lies heavy, like fog, on the spirit, and the thought of the great Arsenius mocks our flagging spirit. Our watching seems to be a bit of muddled reverie before the Lord. Happily our watching more often is a quiet being-with the Loved One, a deep sense that this is right, that this is satisfying to some deep emptiness within. He is coming—it is good to be watching and waiting.

This experiential sense of watching and of the goodness of it usually does not come at once. The novice may be fortunate enough to have a period of honeymoon excitement when the watch is all sweetness and consolation. Or he may not. Soon enough it is fidelity to a practice, an observance, that carries the watcher on. But it is a fidelity that is in time rewarded. Maybe at first only sporadically, but in time it becomes a state of soul, something precious, not all that easy to describe, but precious and prized. It is a restive resting that has its painful delight. It is a time of love, a love more anticipated than experienced, perhaps, but a time of love—a very real "living with" an apparently absent and longed-for Lover. These hours of watching come to be among the most prized hours of our day.

But to be practical, most "monks in the world" can hardly hope to adjust the clocks of their lives so as to be able to rise at the "seventh hour" of the night to enjoy a predawn watch. At best, with careful planning and the sure knowledge that there will be days when it just won't work out, one can plan to retire early enough to have a reasonable period (you will have to decide what might be "reasonable" for you: fifteen minutes, half an hour, an hour?) to "watch" before get-

ting into the usual morning routine. It might be set off with lighting a candle or a bit of incense, a prostration before a holy image, or the enthroned Scriptures, a reading from the Sacred Text or a psalm to rouse the spirit: Come, let us adore.

Some may find it of value and profit to have a more significant vigil once or twice a week, perhaps on Thursday night with Jesus in Gethsemane. This could take the form of rising a good bit earlier, sacrificing some sleep this one night; or breaking sleep at the seventh hour to join in spirit with the monks and nuns in their monasteries. This might be earlier on Friday night or early Saturday morning, when it would be possible to return to bed for a longer sleep. Missing sleep is not the important thing, though for some this can be a significant ascetical dimension of the practice. More important is the experience of being vigilant in the dark silence when others are not commonly abroad and even the creation has a certain dormancy. There is something about the deepness of that bottoming of nature's daily cycle (even in the city where it might still be punctuated by police sirens, the clatter of garbage collectors and the fights of alley cats) that opens out the deeper recesses of the spirit and lets its truer language surface. At such an hour what does creation do but await the sun? What can we do but await the Son?

> I wait for Yahweh, my soul waits for him—
>> more than a watchman waits for the dawn
>> (Ps 130:5-6).

The spirit of watching can be carried on beyond the actual time of prayer. As we shower and dress we can continue to meditate on some Scripture text, repeat some simple prayer, or simply abide in the Presence, longing for an ever greater presence. A household agreement (something more possible when the children are grown) that allows this to be a time of quiet without chatter or the blare of radio, stereo, or television would greatly facilitate this. The watch could formally be concluded with a bit of family prayer at the breakfast table.

In reading the Fathers of the Church and our twelfth-century Cistercian Fathers, we repeatedly come upon the statement: "One who has experienced this understands what I am talking about; one who has not, let him seek the experience and then he will understand." When I was a young monk I used to be quite annoyed when I came upon such "snobbish" statements. Now I begin to understand. Anyone who has loved will. Just try to get another to understand what you experience in your loved one! The same is true here.

The value and effect of watching can only be known by experience. Even a little watching done regularly not only reveals its significance, but has an effect on one's whole life. In the watching, new dimensions of the soul's natural magnetism toward the Lord begin to reveal themselves and the soul begins to have the joy of drawing the Lord into its cool darkness, radiating the warmth of unseen light. At the same time a certain integrity and unity seem gradually to take more and more hold of the multitudinous strands of life, creating a satisfying and empowering harmony. The whole comes more and more into harmony. The reasons for this could be explored at length: a purification process is being facilitated. The solitary perception is becoming more penetrating as these deeper openings are illuminated by the dark light. A freer, more vigorous spirit that has been strengthened to stand its ground in the struggle with darkness takes a firmer hold on the direction of one's life. The extensive effect of a relatively little investment of yourself and your time in watching will in many ways be surprising. The experience of it is in itself very rewarding and it is a constantly growing experience for those who are faithful to the practice.

Chapter Three
By the Labor of Their Hands

"*T*hen are they truly monks," says Saint Benedict, "when, like the apostles and our fathers, they live by the labor of their hands." It may surprise us that this holy legislator who places so much insistence on prayer holds labor in such high regard. We are rather used to the Mary-Martha dichotomy: Mary sits idly at Jesus' feet while her laboring sister is busy about many things (Lk 10:38-42).

But anyone who has kept a property knows that an environment that recalls one to Eden is not created without much labor indeed. And there are many mouths to feed in a monastery—not just the monks or nuns themselves, but their many guests. Moreover, monasteries are famous for their products: the best of wines and beers; the cheeses, wholesome breads and fruit cakes; the vesture, the finest any church can obtain. Monks have been and remain pioneers in new farming methods and husbandry. Yes, there is a lot of work that goes on around a monastery! These "Marys" are also "Marthas"—if not *busy* about many things, certainly accomplishing many things.

Monks and nuns do not embrace this labor primarily as a part of that primal penance imposed upon a sinful race: By the sweat of your brow you will earn your bread. That is an important aspect of work, and one not to be forgotten. And sometimes it seems more present: on the hot muggy days of June or the biting cold days of January; or when those routine chores—washing dishes, vacuuming hallways, shining windows and weeding the carrots—seem like so much boring drudgery; or truly heavy labor leaves backs aching and muscles sore and tired. But labor existed before the fall. God committed to a sinless Adam and his beautiful helpmate a wonderful garden to tend. And in the cool of evening he came to walk arm in arm with his friends to enjoy that garden that together they were creating.

Sometimes we tend to think of creation as a once-and-for-all sort of thing. For six days or six millions years, for however long, God labored and brought forth all that is, and now he rests. It is all done. Not so! At every moment this world and all that is in it comes forth from the loving creativity of an all-good God. This is why our prayer can be

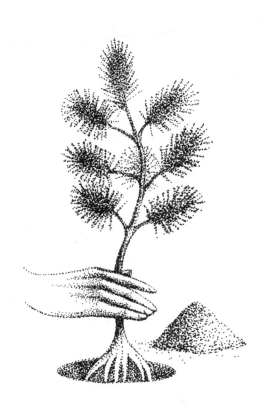

efficacious. Our good God has decided that how he brings forth this creation the next hour, the next day, and on into the future, will depend in part upon our prayer, what we seek and ask. Ask and you shall receive, seek and you will find.

And God is not alone in his world creativity. He has decided that we will be his partners in this project. All our labors are expressions of his creative love. It is he who gives us our physical strength and our knowledge, the intellectual powers to guide the use of our strength, and the will to use these God-given gifts. He is ever present to us and at work with us and in us. All our work is a collaboration with God in bringing his and our creation to its proper fullness.

This is where we monastics find such joy in our work, and know its true dignity, however humble that work might first appear. This is why in all that we do we seek to create something truly beautiful, the finest possible. We build beautiful monasteries and create beautiful settings for them, we seek to produce the finest products in our field. We are working with God to bring forth a new earth, a better world. All things are ours and we are Christ's and Christ is God's. Our work is one with Christ's redeeming work, healing a wounded earth, serving our wounded brothers and sisters. Today's heightened sensitivity to environment, our renewed ecological awareness is certainly a step in the right direction, a rightness that monastic ventures have always proclaimed.

But there is something more, and it is here where the bond of labor with prayer is more intimate. Though obviously a sense of working with God and with Christ in creating and re-creating already makes our work a thing of prayer or union and communion with God. But Saint Benedict opens another perspective for us when he tells us monks and nuns that we are to treat our tools as we would the vessels of the altar. This is not just a wise householder wanting the tools to be well cared for so that they will be kept in good working condition and will last as long as possible. In laboring we celebrate the mass of creation. It is through the work of our human hands that inanimate creation and even sentient creation are elevated to become a sacrifice of praise to our God. In bringing things to their perfection, not just nature and the environment, but intellectual projects and business projects, all kinds of work, we are allowing the universe to sing its hymn ever more beautifully and more fully.

There need be no dichotomies in our lives. It doesn't have to be "either/or." It can be and is of its nature "both/and": both prayer and work. And it is not just a question of a practice of tacking prayer on to our work, though moments of heightened consciousness when we lift our minds and hearts deliberately to God are precious and most desirable. Our work itself, as a collaborative effort with the Creator, is intrinsically prayer, communion with the Divine. Our realization of this will multiply our joy and give us a greater appreciation of our labors, even the most humdrum and routine ones, the ones that seem to be most obviously a part of that primal sentence to penance.

Then are we truly Christians, other Christs, one with Christ, like the apostles and our fathers, when we labor to heal this creation and bring it to the fullness originally intended by our all-good and loving Creator.

Chapter Four
Let Them Devote Themselves to Their Reading

W hat do monks do when they are not about work: the Work of God and the work of creation? They, of course, have all the human cares to attend to. Saint Benedict allows for seven hours of sleep. And a siesta when the season is warm. There is time to eat and time to wash. There is time to be together as brothers or sisters and to receive instruction from the spiritual father or mother. But for the most part, when the monastics are not at work, Benedict's directive is: Let them devote themselves to their reading.

We can not truly enter into the work of God—or any kind of prayer—or, in an appreciative way, into the work of creation without faith. It is by faith that we perceive the Divine Presence, that we know the goodness and love of our God, that we want to praise and worship him and join with him in his creative work. The Scriptures tell us that the just person lives by faith. And faith comes through hearing.

The place we hear the word of faith most powerfully is in the Christian assembly, when we come together to celebrate in one way or another the Word of God. Then Jesus Christ again proclaims his good news. When we hear the Scriptures read in the assembly of the faithful it is God speaking to us and, as we listen, he engenders in us an ever deeper faith.

We can enliven the faith in each other, also, by sharing the word of faith that we have received and that lives within us. It seems a bit strange how difficult it is for some Christians to share faith. They readily talk about anything else: sports, weather, politics, business, but shyly hold back from speaking about what is deepest within them, most meaningful in their lives. There seems to be a conspiracy of silence engendered by I know not what evil spirit. May we learn that generosity which will inspire us to share this our greatest treasure, the one for which the wise person is ready to sell all that he has.

The way that is most readily open to us to hear the word of faith and hear it most intimately is in our own personal reading. Monks and nuns are given more than a few hours each day for reading. Their reading of choice is the divinely inspired Scriptures. Here God himself most directly and immediately speaks to them. If they turn to other writers, it is to women and men of faith who through their writings share their faith and the insights they themselves have received as they read the Scriptures. We realize the need of this. If we are to be ever more conscious of what we are about as we sing God's praises in the church and send up praise to him in our labors, our faith needs to be constantly nurtured. So we devote ourselves to our reading.

The Word that Saint Benedict uses here to speak of reading is a word consecrated by the living tradition. *Lectio* means a special kind of reading. In fact there are different kinds of reading we need in our lives.

We need sacred study, the reading that is meant primarily to enlighten the mind. Faith seeks understanding. We are to love the Lord our God with our whole mind (Mk 12:30). We need ever to "push our edges," to penetrate more deeply into the wonderful realities that our God has so kindly revealed to us through the Scriptures and through the living Tradition of the Church. We need to keep up to date. What is the Spirit saying to the Church, to us today? We cannot expect the Spirit to work in our lives through yesterday's theology. We want to be mature and knowledgeable Christians.

But it is not enough to know. We need to do, to live what we know. So we need another kind of reading: motivational reading. I think this is what most people are talking about when they speak of "spiritual reading," though I am not too sure why they call it "spiritual" reading, for it certainly pertains to the whole of our lives—and we are not spirits! We are very incarnate humans. In any case, what we know in our minds does not always move our heart. Sometimes the insights we receive as we study, especially if we depend very much on the Holy Spirit as we study, are sufficiently powerful in themselves and immediately move us to conversion and renewed action in faith. But sometimes we need some more help to bring the mind down into the heart, to transform our knowledge into action. This is the role of motivational reading. It is reading for the will, for action, for living.

But it is to neither of these kinds of reading that Saint Benedict is referring when he speaks of *lectio*, or, as it is sometimes called, *lectio divina*. In *lectio* we do not seek so much to enlighten the mind or to move the will. Rather we seek the immediate experience of God. We seek to be present to God, who is present in his inspired Word, and let him speak directly to us. It is a direct, immediate encounter with our Friend, our Guide, our Teacher, whom we love.

As the monk comes to his time of *lectio*, the first thing he does is take a moment to realize the real Presence in the sacred Text. Our Bible is one of our most precious possessions. We do not want to put it on the shelf or leave it lying on the table just like all the other books. We want to enthrone it in our room, for it is a Real Presence. Being very aware that our Lord is truly present in his Word, we usually begin our *lectio* by kneeling down, worshiping the Lord. Then we call upon the Holy Spirit, who inspired this Text and who dwells in us to teach us—at the Last Supper Jesus told us this is so—asking the Spirit to help us now to truly hear and learn, to effectively experience the presence of God in his Word.

After this, we sit quietly and listen to the Lord speak

to us through the words of the Text. Sometimes the very first word strikes us and we just sit with it, or rather sit with the Lord in the sharing of that word. We are in no hurry. It is not a question of getting through so much of the text: a page or a chapter. It is rather a question of just being with the Lord and letting him speak to us here and now through these inspired words. Monks and nuns usually sit with their *lectio* until a bell rings, summoning us to the next thing the Lord wants us to do. Since you are not expecting any bells to ring for you, you might want to set a time for yourself. Five or ten minutes might be enough. The Lord does not need a lot of time to get his message across to us. But it is sitting with a Friend who loves us very much. You might, indeed, want to prolong the time. Be that as it may, it is good to have a practice of each day spending a minimal amount of time this way, letting the Lord nourish our faith, so that our prayer and our work will be more satisfying.

At the end of our time of *lectio* we thank the Lord. It is wonderful, isn't it? We can get almighty God himself to sit down and talk with us whenever we want! And we take something along with us: a word, a sentence, a phrase that has especially spoken to us. We keep coming back to it as we go on through the tasks of the day, letting it shed its light on what we are doing. The other day, at the end of my *lectio* I chose the word: I am the way (Jn 14:6). Later as I was walking down the road, I realized that I was not just walking down the street. I was walking in the way, the way that leads all the way to heaven. Then one of the brothers came to me to share a problem that he was faced with. I listened, won-

dering how I would respond. Then I thought: I am the way. The Lord was the answer for him and for his present problem. As the day wore on, I was feeling very tired. I began to wonder how I could get through all I had yet to do. Then I thought: I am the way. And I realized I had a divine Helper with all his strength at my disposal, and we sailed through the rest of the day—together.

This is the way of *lectio*: Sitting down with the Lord and, with the help of his ever present Spirit, letting him give us for this day a word of life. And then letting that word be with us as we walk on through the day, illuminating with the light of Christ all that we do. Living this way, we are truly Christians: disciples of Christ Jesus, letting him be our true master and teacher as well as our savior and friend.

We can sum up this very traditional way of daily meeting our Lord in this way:

Keeping the Sacred Scriptures enthroned in our home in a place of honor as a real Presence in our midst:

> 1. We take up the Sacred Text with reverence, realize that God is present in his Word and call upon the Holy Spirit to help us really hear what he has to say to us *now*.
> 2. For at least five minutes we listen to our Lord speaking to us through the Text and respond to him.
> 3. At the end of our time of *lectio*, we choose a word or phrase that he has "spoken" to us to

take with us and we thank the Lord for being with us and speaking to us.

If each day we can come to the Lord this way and receive a "word" from him, then we will truly be his disciples. His word will color and enrich our lives. We will come to have the mind of Christ, to see things the way he sees them, to do always the things that please the Father, to be true to who we really are as women and men baptized into Christ.

Obviously, if we want to keep God in our lives this way, we have to choose a time that will really work for us for this daily encounter. We need to be very practical about this. My aunt and uncle have their time of *lectio* together at the breakfast table each morning. When you have been together for fifty-five years and are enjoying the leisure of retirement, this shared *lectio* can work very well. I am sure this would be a real possibility for many people. More practical though is something I found among the Christians in Missouri. They enthrone the Bible on their bed pillow. When they are about to retire, they have to pick it up. And they take that time to listen to the Lord, gather a word to reflect upon as they go to sleep, and place the Bible on their shoes. When they rise in the morning, they again have to pick up the Bible. Again, they listen for a bit and take a word to carry with them through the day before re-enthroning the Bible on their pillow. Very practical! and effective. Use your own creativity to find the time and place where you can each day most fruitfully enjoy this encounter with the Lord. It is our tremendous privilege to be the sons and daughters of the Book. To neglect this gift even for a day may not be rank ingratitude but it is foolishness. The just person lives by faith. And that faith needs its daily nourishment just as much as the body needs its. For most of us, it is a rare occasion when we go a whole day without feeding our bodies. How about feeding our Christ-selves as regularly and as well. The monk and the nun usually have several hours at their disposal each day for this feeding. Be good to yourself and each day give yourself at least five or ten minutes to nourish your Christ-life. The just person lives by faith. And faith comes through hearing—hearing the Word of God.

Chapter Five
I Will Refresh You

As I mentioned at the beginning of the last chapter, if the monk or nun is not working or taking care of human needs, physical or social, then Saint Benedict directs them to turn to lectio. I have left that word in the Latin because, as you have seen, it refers to a particular kind of "reading." We don't just read. We enter into a very real and personal contact with the Lord, present in his Word, and listen to him. I have left it in the Latin for another reason. It is a very special word for monks and nuns. When we hear the word lectio, we don't just think of "reading," albeit a very special kind of experiential reading. For us it denominates a whole process, if you will. Or a way of life. When we hear *lectio*, we hear also *meditatio*, *oratio*, and *contemplatio*.

Meditatio: As we mentioned, at the end of the time we have set aside for *lectio* we choose a word or phrase to carry with us as we move on into our day's activities. This is what *meditatio* means here: letting that word we have received in our *lectio* be present within us, perhaps even repeating itself quietly. It is the way in which the Lord, with whom we have sat during our *lectio*, walks on with us through the day. His word continues to illuminate us, cast new light on what we are doing, give us new understanding. He continues to speak to us through it, and in this way be with us as we move on through the day's activities. "I am the way." In him we walk and move and have our being. He has the answers. He is our strength and our consolation. He is the way.

Oratio: As we walk with him, in his "word," we talk with him. This is *oratio*. The word, what we are experiencing, and the light the word casts on this, calls forth from us all sorts of responses. We thank, we praise, we seek more light, we question.... We are two friends, albeit Teacher and disciple, God and his created one. Together we face the journey and all that it brings. This living out of *lectio* can certainly transform our life.

But life does go on. And it makes its many demands; its ceaseless demands. We do grow weary. The burdens are many. Then we hear his word: Come to me, all you who labor and are heavily burdened, and I will refresh you (Mt 11:28). This is the invitation to *contemplatio*. Though we do not nec-

LECTIO
MEDITATIO
ORATIO
CONTEMPLATIO

essarily have to wait until we are weary before we enter into contemplation. During our *lectio* the Lord may as it were invite us to just dwell quietly in the reality with him. *Contemplatio* is the completion of *lectio* we have really heard with our whole being and our whole being responds. It is the complete "yes." *Contemplatio* is the complete *oratio*: beyond words and thoughts. We just simply "are" with the Lord.

For us monks, we have very ample periods of the day which are set apart for *lectio*. The understanding is that as we sit there with the Lord, listening to him speaking to us through his Word, he might at any moment invite us not just to respond in words (*oratio*) but to respond with our whole being, to rest in him, to enter into *contemplatio*. If your periods of lectio are kept quite short, this can hardly happen. Yet your weary spirit does need to respond to the Lord's most gracious invitation: come to me, you who labor and are heavily burdened, and I will refresh you. Indeed, the deepening beckoning of love calls us to simply be with the One whom we love. For this reason Tradition does give us a simple method which we can use at any time to enter into contemplative rest with the Lord we love. But in order to be properly refreshed we will probably have to insure ourselves of at least fifteen or twenty minutes, in a place where we can feel comfortably free that we will not be disturbed and can just let go and be with our Lord within.

"Within"—our God of course is everywhere. But in a very special way, the Father, Son and Spirit do dwell within us. Jesus told us this on the night before he died: The Father and I will come and we will make *our home* in you.

God is everywhere, but where does he dwell in intimacy with the ones he loves? Within us, each one of us, at the heart, the center of our being. This is why this prayer has been called "Prayer in the Heart" or "Centering Prayer."

In response to his word, in faith and with love, we turn to him within and gently rest—not thinking, or feeling, or imagining, or speaking, or promising, or.... Just being with—being with the One we love. And who loves us.

In order to stay quietly there with him, we use a little word of love. Choose whatever word you will: God, Love, Jesus, Lord, Friend.... We do not have to repeat this word all the time we are resting with the Lord. We just use it as much as we need to, to stay quietly with him within.

Of course, the mind keeps chattering, the imagination keeps showing pictures, the emotions tug us this way and that, the memory has its stories to tell, etc. It is amazing how much goes on within us. No wonder we are so tired at the end of each day. But during this time of resting with the Lord, we just let all that go on on its own. We don't give it the least bit of attention. If it seeks to grab our attention, we gently return to the Lord, using our little word of love. Some days we have to use that word almost without ceasing—things just keep pulling at us. No matter. As long as we use the word most gently, we will nonetheless be refreshed.

This is the simple method of prayer that old Abba Isaac taught Saint John Cassian way back in the fifth century. Saint John wrote down what Abba Isaac taught him. Later, when Saint Benedict wrote his Rule he advised his monks to go to Saint John for instruction on prayer. Thus this little method for entering into *contemplatio* became the common way of prayer for multitudes of monks and nuns through the centuries. And they frequently taught it to those who came to them for guidance. In the earliest days of the English language a spiritual father (whose name we do not know) wrote a little book about this kind of prayer for his spiritual son which became quite famous: *The Cloud Of Unknowing.*

I have found that it is good to end our time of contemplation very gently. That is why I recommend (this is not from Abba Isaac but from Abba Basil) that at the end of the time you have set apart for resting in the Lord, you don't end your prayer abruptly but, leaving aside your love word, you let the prayer Jesus taught us gently pray itself within. I have found that often during this time the Lord brings to my mind many things, many insights that are helpful. I can see now how saints have been able to write whole books on the Lord's Prayer.

So let me now sum up this little traditional method of entering into *contemplatio*:

After you get settled comfortably, with your eyes gently closed and your feet set firmly on the floor, your back well supported—so the body can rest even as the spirit does:

1. Be in faith and love to God who dwells in the center of your being.

2. Take up your love word and fix it in your mind, supporting your being to God in faith-filled love.

3. Whenever you become aware of anything else, simply, gently, return to the Lord with the use of your love word.

At the end of the time you have set aside (fifteen or twenty minutes) let the Lord's Prayer quietly pray itself within.

In our monastery here we sit together twice a day in this kind of prayer. Being together we really support each other in the prayer. I am sure you will find it helpful if you can get others to pray with you this way. Just sitting there together in the silence we give a strong witness to each other of our common faith.

If we pray this way twice a day, very quickly our whole life becomes more centered, more free. Those fruits of the Spirit, which Saint Paul speaks of in his Letter to the Galatians, begin to be more and more present in our lives; love, joy, peace, patience, kindness, gentleness, long-suffering, chastity (Gal 5:9). By these fruits, as our Lord said, you will know what a wonderful prayer this is. Indeed, we will be refreshed.

Chapter Six
The Tranquility of Order

S o the monk's life is filled with liturgy, labor and that lectio which culminates in contemplative rest in the Lord. The three "L"s are all directed to the Lord and come together in him. It is a tripod well grounded in a fully human life, rich in friendship and fraternal support. The three are blended together in such wise that each supports the other; a balance is preserved. There is no stress or strain or feverish activity in this monastic life. There is peace, the tranquility of order.

Why did God make us? Oh, I know, the catechism has its answer, not really the best of answers. Indeed, one that could be misleading and lead us to misunderstand God and even rebel against him. The idea of a God who wants us only to serve him here, promising some happiness later on somewhere in the sky—that is not a very attractive God. And it is not our God.

Our God is three, three divine persons, who are forever celebrating the oneness of their love and the wonder of each other in that absolute oneness. They are always totally happy, an eternal celebration of love. And what do you want to do when you are really happy? Share it. And that is why God made us. He wanted someone with whom he could share his immense, overflowing happiness.

But what is happiness? I am sure you have your own definitions for that. But try this out, and see if it is not a good one: Happiness consists in knowing what you want, and then knowing you have it or you are on the way to getting it.

Do you remember what are the first recorded words of Jesus to his disciples? You remember the story, an oft repeated one: Two fine young men, working with their families, fishermen on the banks of the Sea of Galilee. They knew that there had to be something more. Then one day they headed East. They heard there was someone special out there: a strange sort of fellow, wearing a camel's coat and chewing on grasshoppers. They went and asked him: Are you the One? The Baptizer was a humble man: No, I am not he. But wait around; he is coming. And so they waited. And then one day, as the Baptizer was about his business, he suddenly looked up and pointed: There, there is the Lamb of God. And the two fishermen, Andrew and John, took off.

As they ran up behind Jesus he turned to them—and here we have his first recorded words to his disciples: What do you want? (Jn 1:38). Happiness is knowing what we want and knowing we have it or are on the way to getting it.

A monk's life is very, very happy. That is why there is so much joy and peace around a monastery. Monks know what they want. And to some extent they already have it. More important, they know the way of life they are following will inevitably lead to enjoying it to the full.

But how does someone who does not lead such a privileged life bring such order and direction into his or her life in our all too frenetic world. The one who plans a thing succeeds, says the Book of Proverbs. We need to bring that peace and order from within. Otherwise we find ourselves always doing the immediate and never doing the important. The monk has the privilege of living according to a well-tried Rule that benefits from the wisdom of the centuries. You have to construct your own rule of life.

Some people do not like the idea of rules. They think of them as restrictive, as cages, which in the end inhibit the freedom of the Spirit and impede growth. I think it is better to see a rule of life as a trellis. If you give a climbing rose a trellis, it can do what it really wants to do, climb toward the sun and bear a thousand blossoms. Without the trellis it becomes a rather dead heap. But note, the climbing rose, so full of life, is usually away from the trellis. But when it starts to fall back, the trellis is there to support it. So too with your rule of life. Much of the time

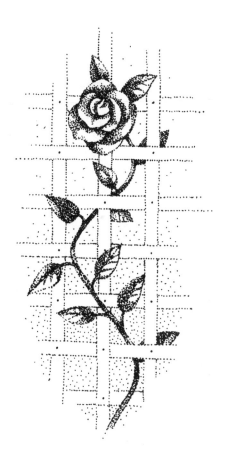

you will be away from it; your life is full and active and going in many directions. But it is ever there to support you in basically doing what you want to do, going in the direction you want to go, the way to happiness.

To construct your rule you want to call upon the Spirit. The Spirit knows where the fullness of your happiness lies: Eye has not seen, nor ear heard, nor has it entered into the human mind what God has prepared for those who love him, but the Holy Spirit makes it known to us (1 Cor 2:9).

Depending on the Spirit, we first need to ask ourselves what the Lord has first asked: What do you want? As humans there are certain things we definitely want. Happiness begins with going to bed—for we will never be happy if we don't get enough sleep. And we need food, exercise, friends, intellectual stimulation, etc. But we are more than human. We have been baptized into Christ and so we also need the things of Christ-life: prayer, sacraments, Scripture, etc. And there are those things we want because we want them; the choices of our freedom.

Knowing what we want, we then need to take a practical inventory of what we need to do to get the things we want. We can be helped in this by taking a look over our shoulder and asking: what has been preventing me from getting what I want, being who I want to be? Maybe now is the time for the serenity prayer:

> Lord, give me the serenity to accept the things I can't change, the courage to change the things I can change, and the wisdom to know the difference.

With all this data we are now ready to construct our own rule of life on a daily, weekly and monthly basis. At least once a month it is good to take time out for a bit of retreat, to "re-treat" again our rule and see how things are going. Some things we do more on a weekly rhythm: exercise three or four times a week, have a good time with our friends, take time out for some serious study, etc. Other things are daily needs: sleeping, eating, *lectio* and labor....

This is a challenging moment. I am afraid most of us find that there are far more things we want to do than can possibly fit into a twenty-four-hour day and a seven-day week. We have to make choices. This is good. Consciously giving up some good things in order to do others, we will do the chosen things with a much greater fullness and find a greater joy in them. Moreover, really making choices and letting go of some of the multitude of desires that have been lurking within us, we let go of some of the simmering unhappiness that has been lurking within us because of these unfilled desires. Our energies are released to be devoted joyfully to the pursuit of what we really want.

Creating a rule of life like this is a simple enough exercise, though it can be a very demanding one. It opens the way to a much greater clarity and joy in our lives. It brings us that tranquility of order, which we call peace.

Chapter Seven

Welcome Again

Yes, welcome again, and again, and again. A thousand welcomes. You are always most welcome at a monastery.

Saint Benedict provides that there should always be at the gate of the monastery a wise old man, one with the benignity of years who knows how to give a hearty and warm welcome. There is always to be a guesthouse, one well provided and carefully kept. Especially is the stranger and traveler to be welcomed. For it is the Lord.

I have always been struck at the way our Lord describes the last judgment. He does not say anything about our prayers and contemplation, nor about our labor and our *lectio.* Rather he speaks about feeding and giving drink, about welcoming and clothing, about visiting (Mt 25).

That fact is, though, that our monasteries are usually far from the city streets where the homeless and hungry are to be found. Few of them find their way to our door far out in the country. What then are monks to do?

Well, we certainly welcome anyone who does come to our door. But that certainly is not enough. What most monasteries do is ally themselves with a Catholic Worker home or some other shelter in the city. The monastery becomes the spiritual home of those servants of the poor who live and labor in the midst of the city with all its imperious demands. These men and women are ever welcome and can find at the monastery the rest and refreshment they need so that they will not burn out in the course of their demanding and important ministry. At the same time the monks and nuns may well plant some acres of vegetables for the poor, to be distributed through their city allies. They share the fruit of their labor in whatever way they can. Their outreach may be remote but their heart with its love, its care, its concern is right there with the poor and needy. We are one in Christ.

You may very well be in much the same situation as the monks and nuns. Christ in the poor may rarely if ever come to your door. And if he or she does, you perhaps have little or no room to give shelter. But you can reach out. There is undoubtedly not too far from you some shelter, soup kitchen, or pantry for the poor which can receive your attention and give you an opportunity to feed and clothe and shelter the poor Christ. If there is not, then you might well take the initiative to call forth friends and neighbors to establish one. And you can begin to visit Christ in the hospital or prison. Most parishes have a unit of the Legion of Mary or some other group that undertakes this ministry.

> Come, possess the kingdom that was prepared for you ever since the creation of the world. For I was hungry and you fed me, thirsty and you gave me to drink. I was a stranger and you received me into your home, naked and you clothed me; I was sick and you took care of me, in prison and you visited me (Mt 25:34-36).

Our Lord has told us that we are to judge a tree by its fruit. We can tell that our "hours," our watching, our labor, our *lectio*, our contemplation is what it should be if we are, in a way that is in accord with our own particular vocation, effectively living in solidarity with the poor Christ, with Christ in the poor.

> Whatever you do for the least of mine, you do for me (Mt 25:40).

We cannot ignore the poor and needy without at the same time ignoring Christ, our Lord and Savior.

Goodbye for Now

Goodbye for now. And next time when you see a monastery off on a hill or down in the valley, do drop in. You might join us for one of the hours, or just for a cup of tea. And take along with you some of our products: some cookies, or candy, or Trappist preserves.

Or you might like to take along a book. I have written a number of books that fill out the little bit that I have shared with you here:

Light from the Cloister: A Practical Spirituality for Practical Christians Inspired by Monastic Practice (Paulist Press)

The Monastic Way (Crossroad)

Called: New Thinking on Christian Vocation (Seabury)

Daily We Touch Him: Practical Religious Experiences (Doubleday)

Centering Prayer: Renewing an Ancient Christian Prayer Form (Doubleday)

Centered Living: The Way of Centering Prayer (Doubleday)

Call to the Center (Doubleday)

Jubilee: A Monk's Journal (Paulist)

O Holy Mountain: Journal of a Retreat on Mount Athos (Liturgical Press)

In Search of True Wisdom: Visits to Eastern Spiritual Fathers and Mothers (Alba House)

A Manual of Life: The New Testament for Daily Reading (Paulist Press)

Thomas Merton, Brother Monk: The Quest for True Freedom (HarperCollins)

Prayertimes: Morning–Midday–Evening: A Pocket "Liturgy of the Hours" for All Christians (Doubleday)

A Retreat with Thomas Merton (Continuum Books)

Through the Year with the Saints: A Daily Companion for Private or Liturgical Prayer (Doubleday)

Awake in the Spirit: A Personal Handbook on Prayer (Doubleday)

Goodbye for now. And thanks for allowing me to share with you. Do say a prayer for me and my brothers and sisters in the monastery. And we will be praying for you.

Other Books in the Series

Little Pieces of Light...Darkness and Personal Growth
   by Joyce Rupp

Spirituality, Stress & You
   by Thomas E. Rodgerson

As You and the Abused Person Journey Together
   by Sharon E. Cheston